Arthur Compton-Rickett

Lost Chords

Some Emotions Without Morals

Arthur Compton-Rickett

Lost Chords
Some Emotions Without Morals

ISBN/EAN: 9783744692847

Printed in Europe, USA, Canada, Australia, Japan

Cover: Foto ©Thomas Meinert / pixelio.de

More available books at **www.hansebooks.com**

To my Father.

CONTENTS.

	PAGE
HARMONIES IN YELLOW—	
Miss Maud's Three Notes	11
A Yellow Creeper	17
Golden Syrup	24
A Bass Fugue	27
Pose Fancies	34
FANTASIE—	
Cinquante Ans Après	45
A Christmas Mixture	56
The New Cinderella	62
How to be a Dramatic Critic	68
The Game of Interviewing	75
Through the (Political) Looking-Glass	82
AIRS—	
The Modern Young Man to his Love	93
Seasonable Thoughts	95
Locksley Hall (during Spring Cleaning)	97
Pillow Philosophy	99
To Pickwick	102
The Poets at School	104
Reflections of a Poetaster	110

Some of the following sketches are now appearing for the first time; many, however, have already appeared in The Granta, The Globe, The Cambridge Review, Lika Joko, *and a school magazine. My thanks are due to the present Editors of* The Granta, *Editors of* The Cambridge Review, *Mr. R. C. Lehmann, the Editor of* The Globe, *Mr. Harry Furniss, and the Editors of* The Cinque Port, *for their courtesy in permitting me to reprint the same.*

ARTHUR RICKETT.

100, Lancaster Gate, London, W.

HARMONIES IN YELLOW.

I

MISS MAUD'S THREE NOTES.

(Dedicated to the Author of "Keynotes," "Discords.")

THE FIRST NOTE.

IT was a fat book with green covers.

"Huxley's Outlines of Physiology," shouted Maud, joyously. "Hurrah!"

She had been washing the family linen in a back room, and the sight of this romantic work affected her wonderfully.

"Happy at last," gurgled Maud again, pushing some straggling brown hairs off her marbly brow.

The blue veins in the white neck swelled out distinctly, like broad beans.

She rocked her slight, girlish figure to and fro, and hugged the book to her palpitating breast.

"I think Mister Halfred 'as lost a green book, if you please, Miss Maud." It was the butler. Butlers always speak like that.

"Man," hissed Maud, with all the scorn of eighteen summers, "shall I be deprived of reading a book that my brother is familiar with? Never!" The roses came and went in her cheeks.

She kicked a slipper off her pretty foot, and it hit the butler on the head.

"Your slipper, I believe, Miss!" said the servant, imperturbably, handing it back.

"I spurn that toy of convention," shrieked Maud. Then she put on a pair of Wellingtons, and strode out into the back garden.

The Second Note.

Greedily she drank in the sweet, warm air of June.

The bees were humming; the sun setting; the wind-distended garments of a neighbour flapped over the wall.

The perfume of honeysuckle came borne on the breeze, together with that of refuse from a dust-heap.

Maud stood on the lawn lecturing an old tabby on the largeness of her family. "You should read Malthus, Pussy," she whispered.

The cat viewed her with soft, brown, blinking eyes; then peered anxiously forward.

"Puss," said Maud, with nervous energy, "what are you thinking of?" Pussy pounced at a small bird.

"O—o—h!" murmured Maud. She was bitterly disappointed, but was too proud to show it; she had imagined that some vague feline ideal . . . But it hadn't. The cat was but an unimaginative creature with gross appetites.

Maud scooped up the damp earth with her slender fingers. "I *do* want to shock somebody" (with a petulant drawl), "and it's so hard nowadays."

The sound of a voice came borne on the west wind.

Surely it was the bestial, monotonous, and rattling sound of a man snoring, or a pig grunting.

THE THIRD NOTE.

The old gardener was sleeping in the cucumber frame.

Maud had a wonderful eye for detail, and the picture was impressed upon her mind.

A red, swollen, pimply face, with violet eyelids. A short, broad, vermilion nose. Thick crimson lips tinged with blue. The beard was stubby and unkempt, and the blotchy patches of green skin shone through the coarse grey hair. The grubby collar and worn brown shirt were stained with tobacco juice. A tin bottle lay by his side.

"What a brute man looks asleep," commented Maud, and threw a flower-pot at him. It fell considerably wide of the mark, but it aroused the sleeping monster, who opened his eyes and used bad words.

"Is that always what you men say when you are vexed?" and the girl's white nostrils dilated with scorn.

"Noa, noa," growled the gardener, in a raspy dialect. "I swears when I likes a thing just the same as I swears when I don't likes a thing."

"I feel," said Maud, "I don't know—I can't express—I hate men; I loathe men. I don't know why, but I do. They are so brutal, have such thick lips and bleary eyes. . . . Are so sensual, boorish, cruel . . . so *everything*, in fact "—with fierce energy—" whilst women are so delicate, wonderful, emotional, Æolian Harpist . . . and all that," with vague enthusiasm. "Where do you live, O swinish man?" said the sensitive, nerve-racked girl, clasping and unclasping her long, slender fingers.

"Middlesex," between bluish-grey-brown clouds of smoke.

"Sex!" screamed Maud (she had got her cue). "Sex! Ah, that word! What is it, I should like to know? Where is it?"

"Where isn't it?" grunted the brute.

These discussions with his young mistress were the usual thing each afternoon.

"Sex is a mystery," said Maud.

"Shouldn't have thought it to have heard you talk," snarled the brute. "But you'll excuse me, miss—I'm a respectable married man with nine children, and I don't feel it decent to be a-talkin' with a chit like you about these 'ere things."

"An advanced girl of eighteen . . . a chit— you, you——" she almost choked with passion. "Why it's in the air, it's——"

"There's a strong smell o' drains in the

air," said the brute, "and I advise you to run in."

. . . . .

How still she was; the violence of her passion had convulsed her, leaving her pale and breathless. "Shall I kill him?" She clenched her fists, till the blood spurted from the palms. "No," in a low, awful voice, "I will do worse. I will write a book for a series"—and she was another woman who did.

II.

A YELLOW CREEPER.

(Dedicated to the Author of "The Great God Pan, and the Inmost Light.")

THE Doctor poured a green fluid into a phial containing red fluid: then he poured, very carefully, something black into the mixture, and held up, as the result of the foregoing process, a clear, limpid, crystal-like fluid.

"How do you manage that?" said the friend.

"I don't quite know," replied the Doctor, thoughtfully. "You see, I proceed by an intuitive process, shutting my eyes and taking the first bottle that comes. Great experiments defy the arbitrary rules of scientific formulæ. You, my friend, shall share this great discovery with me."

"Shall I?" said the friend, without enthusiasm. He was only an ordinary man, and connected discoveries with Government duty.

"Certainly," asserted the Doctor. "Here, smell this mixture; it has an exquisite aroma."

"Hum—well—rather peculiar, isn't it?" said the friend, sniffing doubtfully at the crystal fluid. "Rather reminds me of the decayed remains of Hawthorne and Edgar Allen Poe.

"Bah!" snapped the Doctor, "I ought to have remembered that the nostril of the unimaginative man is lacking in delicate appreciation."

"I always had an unreasonable dislike of anything mouldering," sighed the ordinary friend, "but I may improve in course of time."

The Doctor put down the phial and took up a glass rod. "You'll excuse my putting out the light."

"Where was Moses——" commenced the ordinary friend to cheer himself up, but a scowl from the other quenched him.

A faint phosphorescent gleam came from the crystal fluid.

A YELLOW CREEPER.

"You doubtless know," observed the scientist, with gusto, "that the chemical constituent R_2OT_3 reacts on its agent $P_4IFF_5LE_6$ so as to re-combine and deposit a neutral acid-alkaline——"

"Excuse me," said the ordinary friend, modestly, "but I only took a Poll degree,"

"Dear me, how unfortunate!" deprecated the Doctor; "the Natural Science Tripos made me the man I am. The practical papers aroused in me a passion for experiment which will make me a nuisance to every one for the rest of my life. However, I will omit the scientific explanation. Watch me. I take this glass in my right hand and the globules in my left——"

The mind of the ordinary friend began to wander. His memory reverted to childhood's days, and to the annual conjurer at Christmas parties. Then he fell into a troubled sleep, with his head resting on a large bottle of ammonia.

"Wake up!" cried the Doctor, "you will miss the experiment."

"Oh, why did I take lork and pobster?—I mean pork and lobster," gasped the friend, awaking with a start; "I will be a porktotaler after this."

"It is not matter that is affecting you, but spirit," commenced the Doctor. The friend looked indignant, but the other went on. "What I mean is, you are approaching the gurgling mysteries, the ghastly, unspeakable, shuddering mysteries, that dwell in cheap books. Man alive! However can you pass Smith's bookstall without shrinking appalled in large-nosed, white-eared, terror from the hideosities that abound there? How can you do it?"

"Answers to be received by the first post on Monday, written on a postcard," murmured the very ordinary friend. His mind was wandering.

The Doctor gave him up, and returning to his phial, dropped a small quantity of the fluid on a young bluebottle lost in meditation on a plate. For one moment the bluebottle paused stupefied; then it lubricated its legs together with violence, gave a fearful buzz of despair, and turned into an old blowfly. Only for a second. It rapidly became a red-bottle ("Best Scotch"), then an alligator, a scarecrow, a Beardsley poster, and finally dissolved into nothing. All this was viewed by the light of a lucifer.

"This is the dreadful secret of personality," remarked the Doctor. "Thus does the spirit triumph over matter, and disregarding the petty limitations of sense——Blast! . . . ! ! !"
—for the lucifer had burnt down to his fingers.

. . . . .

The ordinary friend got off a 'bus ten years later, and nearly knocked down a man who was getting in.

"You, Jim! How changed you are!"

"Aye," said Jim, with a haggard look (he always said "aye" when he felt unwell. It was more impressive than "yes"). Then seizing the other by the arm, he conveyed him into a "Bodega," feverishly drank off some raw spirit, and muttered, "Excuse my incoherence —married life failure—collect curios—just purchased collection of flies—amongst them bluebottle."

"It's portrait—it's portrait," said the ordinary friend, excitedly.

"Here," said Jim, producing a *carte de visite*. "It has come between me and my wife. Yesterday I saw an alligator in the drawing-room. Last night my wife saw a bottle of Scotch whiskey in my study."

"This is indeed a blue story," said the ordinary friend, "but I know that bluebottle, it comes from the Doctor's laboratory. Kill it, Jim—kill it!"

"I am an anti-vivisectionist," exclaimed Jim, and rushed out, leaving the ordinary friend to pay for the drinks.

. . . . .

I, Doctor Bunkum, have been asked to recount what I saw. My knowledge of the English language is but slight, owing to the excessive attention given in early manhood to the classical subjects in the Little-Go. But I will do my best. When I was called in, the temperature of the room was 212° Fahr., and a green twilight suffused everything. I am a stolid man, but my pulse beat 599 to the minute; yet I retained my self-control.

The thing was buzzing fiercely after a dissipated course of fly-papers. I felt its pulse, and gave it a bottle of influenza mixture. It rapidly grew worse; it resembled a saneless, painless, brainless lump of blue jelly. Neither male nor female, animal, vegetable or mineral. Then it began to dissolve. I have been at the Dissolution of Parliament, but never have I——!! yet words fail!! I crept under a copy of the *Westminster Gazette*, and waited for the finale. No, excuse me, I did not wait, I hurried out, wrote down my impressions for the Public, and then made my will. When these pages are being read, I shall probably be either dead or living!!

III.

GOLDEN SYRUP.

(Dedicated to the Authoress of " Theodora.")

. . . . .

THE next day Garbage rose at 2 p.m. "There is no doubt about it," said he, as he allowed his ivory fingers to twine themselves amongst his brilliantined locks; "the fragment is a most effective and affected form of composition; and when one wishes to out-Ouida Ouida, and out-Egerton Egerton, then . . . "

A few minutes afterwards he was admiring the sensuous curve of the sardines on his breakfast-plate. The thick, silky oil caressed them with a thousand oleaginous embraces; and this filled him with a mad, delicious, ethereal pleasure. Some men would have been stirred in their coarse animal appetites. Not so Garbage;

he regarded sardines from a spiritual standpoint. And yet he was no ascetic, no dyspeptic. He could rejoice in the fierce, biting vinegar and the wildly stinging pepper as well as in the clinging oil. Yet was he a marvel of self-restraint; and his friends wondered greatly when they saw him lazily dividing the silver-grey fish, and languidly removing the backbone to a side of the plate.

"Hello!" said Newdle, who looked upon Garbage with a veneration which was as needless as it was idiotic. "Breakfast at this hour?"

A queer, thin, constrained, unmeaning smile flickered over the mouth of Garbage. All sorts of smart things occurred to him. . . . Alas! when the mind has almost freed itself from the shackles of sense, and enveloped itself in nonsense, then are we reminded, as he was, as we all are, or were, or will be. . . . Garbage sneezed.

At this sign of weakness, Newdle sprang to his feet.

"Garbage, you have been thinking of *her*. You . . . you *like* her! Tell me candidly, frankly —never mind the Philistine—what do you think of her?"

Garbage convulsively pressed his finger to his upper lip, possibly to avoid another sneeze, then he replied—

"Think? Surely, Newdle, you have found out by now that thought is alien to my nature, and nature alien to my thought. I subject my soul to a keen, analytical, subjective, introspective probing. But if you follow me closely, you will know what transcends even thought . . . provided you keep a dictionary by you."

"A fishy story?" queried Newdle, looking at the sardines.

Garbage cracked a boiled egg with fine scorn.

"It is impossible to shock a novel-reader nowadays. You must either tell a story in dialect or—indecently. Only Scotchmen can afford to write cleanly . . . "

At this moment the window blew open, and directly Garbage felt the fresh air he fainted.

.   .   .   .   .

Before he could recover a host of critics rushed into the room, armed with pens of the finest tempered steel.

Mr. H———y Q———r designed the tombstone.

IV.

A BASS FUGUE (MAESTROSO, LARGHISSIMO).

(Dedicated to H. B. M—r—t W—n.)

HE stood on the doorstep with one foot poised on the scraper. A variety of sensations emotionalised him and made him feel he would not have been as he was if he could have been as he might have been. Some men, after a good dinner such as he had enjoyed, might have sat on the doorstep; not so Cyril. Like others of his family, he had, if not an iron will, at least, a wooden head. And yet as he gnawed his toothpick and stared at the knocker, queer thoughts caused his nose to tremble and his ears to waver rhythmically. He tried to forget what had happened: he tried to imagine himself in his easy-chair, in bed, on the Alps, at the North Pole, in the Planet Mars, anywhere but on the steps of his own house, 13, Gromser Gardens, S.W. It was a failure. In shutting his eyes he only managed to knock off his hat. So by the chaste beams of a street lamp he gazed idly into the faces of the passing atoms of humanity. Beneath him lay the ground, overhead was the sky, omnibuses rattled by on wheels, a cat burst into song, and a snail with a past moved uneasily on the doorpost. Yes, the conclusion was forced upon him that the great world was rolling round as usual. And yet, within him—a human man, a biped with two legs—lay a mighty change; beside which the small change in his trouser pocket was as nothing. His mind (unlike his Suéde gloves) was soiled with the memory of a reminiscence. For, was not his wife learning cooking? had she not insisted, with the fanatical fury of an amateur, upon cooking *all* the meals? " It will save a cook, dear, and be so much cheaper, and you will fancy things cooked by your little wifey, won't you ? " " Yes," had been his reply—a reply spoken in the indolent ease of ignorance. Ah! that fatal assent; it had been the beginning of the commencement, the incipiency of all. He had wildly promised, reckless of life, health, and happiness, to save up his appetite during the day, until he could repast off the wife-cooked viands in the evening.

The first day he had kept his promise. Throughout the long hours of the night he had bitterly repented his fidelity. If the path of virtue and truthfulness were strewn with raw meat and leaden pastry, welcome then the path of deceit, unfaithfulness, and gastronomic peace. On this the second day, allured by the smell outside Gatti's of steaming dainties, he had yielded to his natural inclination for a well-cooked dinner, and . . .

So he chewed the toothpick gloomily, whilst the *Roederer* and coffee flowed merrily through his veins.

But it could not last. He gave a postman's knock, and almost broke the bell; then his head fell and his eyes were downcast as he heard a light step the other side. The door opened; he was vaguely aware of the servant's presence.

"Mistress in?" he muttered, with a brusque and elaborate indifference.

"Yes, sir."

Even the servant's voice was altered. Could she read his secret? Ah, there had been onions with the steak. He brushed past her, and put down his hat on the hall table.

"Your name, sir!"

"My name!" What! was he so altered as *that?* He buried his face in his hands. Was it that this new life of deceit and shame had branded him with an alien expression? Too terrible! He raised his head, looked at the servant steadily with an effort, and opened his mouth to speak; then his jaw fell, and he remained silent. It was a new servant.

"When did you come?" said the man.

"What concern is that of yours," said the girl, with hauteur and a rising colour. "Your name?"

"Insolence!" he muttered. "I am your master, girl!"

"Git out, or state yer business. Else I go for master. Imperence!"

She tried to turn up her nose, but nature had given it such a celestial *penchant*, that the feat was impossible. A door opened and there was the rustle of a woman's dress. Cyril rushed forward.

"Winny, what does this mean? Do you hear? . . . Let me . . . " He stopped. A dull, sickening horror seized him. His burning eyes scanned the carpet, the walls, the floor, and the ceiling. The horror became a ghastly reality. The toothpick fell from his mouth. He had got into the wrong house. Then he rushed madly away, tripped over a fat, asthmatic pug dog, and caused it to be laid up for weeks on a bed of suffering. On and down the steps he sped, the ribald laughter from the servant girl and the opprobrious remarks from the mistress following him, and surging in his singing ears.

"This is not a *Truth* story," he shrieked, "it is a serious, dramatic piece of imaginative work; no more anti-climaxes. Ten to one on a good old 'curtain.'"

With these words he sped up the steps of No. 13, a glazed, jaundiced, desperate look in his eyes, like poached eggs at bay.

When in the hall he blew his nose. It was a trumpet-call of challenge to the fates that preside over short stories. A woman, dressed in a soft, clinging, summer-saleish something, glided into the hall.

Hers was no mere ephemeral and common

beauty. Her face was of a rich and bewitching neutral tint, and her complexion suggested culinary analogies with half-baked pastry. There was a bold, arched, imperative significance about her Roman nose; and the seductive curves of the glinting spectacles were indescribable.

Now for it. Grinding his teeth together and dashing his hat into a coal-scuttle, he hissed out, with brutal frankness:

"Winny, I will not deceive you. I have dined!"

There was a dreadful silence, broken only by the sound of the piano-organ playing "She only answered 'Ting-a-ling-a-ling,'" and a passing street arab yelling the music-hall ditty, "That's what I call plucky." Otherwise all was still. Then the woman spoke.

"Well, I'm glad of it, Cyril, for the pipes have gone wrong to-day, so I didn't use the kitchen fire, and I had to get my food out, so I hoped you would do so. But," with a gentle nasal emphasis that added a piquancy to an otherwise monotonous voice, "*I* had a glass of milk with mine."

Cyril leant against the umbrella-stand, and the poached eggs looked more desperate than ever.

"Is that all?" he murmured, in a broken voice. "Am I to understand you refuse to faint, or at least to open your arms, to stagger with a white, ghastly face, and with lines pitiably drawn round your mouth, or to call out 'Cyril' with heart-choking sobs. . . . Oh Winny, I did not expect this of you! This second anti-climax has ruined my life!"

As he spoke, a large, thoughtful-looking smut trembled in the air; and gradually settled down upon his nose.

V.

POSE FANCIES.

(Dedicated to R. Le G—ll—e, author of " Prose Fancies.")

Spring.

I.

SPRING, with that amiable knack she has of pleasing me, has leapt from the bosom of Mother Nature, and is smiling upon us. See! She approaches the young wife, and into her ear breathes a suggestion or two. At the sound a soft, rapt look comes into the eager eyes, and the word "cleaning" floats upon the agitated air. The bedrooms will soon be spangled with innumerable antimacassars, and the brooding beetle will turn a sabler hue at the thought that his doom is nigh. Let us away into the garden, my friend, to seek the vernal beauties of thy small back yard! Turn thy gaze, clouded with the dust of beaten carpets, on to the sluglings that are galloping around in the dewy freshness of youth, and with the mystery of a painless joy writ on their fair young faces. Their quaint *naïveté* recalls the fabled, flying-horse Pegasus, or at least would do so, did they but fly and were they larger in size and faster in speed. Mark the caressing tenderness of the elder slug, the clinging coyness (such as thy white-eyed love was wont to greet thee with) of her embrace, and the grey glory of her delicate moulding.

To my way of thinking there is a strange loss of charm when a slug becomes a silkworm, but in the fleeting hours of slughood she attracts my wayward fancy more than any other bird (excuse, kind reader, the slight inaccuracy, but the word insect is less euphonious). Oh, my friend, crush that dull, prosaic spirit of thine; quell that cynical and worldly contempt! and reverently remove the boots from thy head when the slug, Nature's crawling child, passes upon her pilgrimage.

Why do we not indulge in such delicious

caprices of locomotion? Why brood we not in dusky meditation on the green and cool-veined cabbage? Is it not because we are for ever bent on doing something, because we so foolishly fret ourselves with the eternal monotony of mental activity? Is it not because we are too gross and awkward to rest on the leaf of the cabbage with any degree of comfort?

But—*revenons à nos limaces!*

See, the sluglings are retiring to roost! We must not awake them.

Dry thine eyes, my friend.

Having thus wasted our time so far, let us pass on.

II.

Down in the depths of the old armchair there is an absence of spring, a harshness, that pains the sensitive nerves. Yet, shortly, some upholstering angel will arrive; spring will return once more; the shrunken leather will become smooth and plump, and we shall experience a sense of comfort to which we have long been strangers.

Behold (what were we talking about? Ah, of course, spring)—behold that ancient cabbage—

a study in green and gold; of what is it dreaming? Perchance of the lettuce days of youth, perchance not. In the dark, dank hours of the night I have often wondered and thought, and thought and wondered why a grey-eyed girl asked me, "If a herring and a half cost threepence, how much—many——" But I have forgotten it.

III.

Who threw that rotten apple at me? You say it was that red-nosed town urchin. Fie on thee, child of the city! Yet why fie? Does it not arise from the exuberance of a young child rejoicing in the poetry of rural life? Does not his sweet young cockney accent attract, Orpheus-like, the animal creation? And yet, methinks, Orpheus had no catapault.

IV.

The spring onion has a wonderful way of bringing tears to the eyes. I have seen hard-nosed burly men chewing it with brimful orbits. A spring-gun has a similar effect on the emotions, as I well remember when in the days of long ago that denizen of the woods mistook my nether limbs for a cat.

Àpropos of cats, what an expressive thing is sympathy! Observe, for instance, how, at election times, like sleep in Coleridge's golden lines, it is
"Beloved from poll to poll."

Surely it is not given to every man to discourse so daintily on spring.

On Books and Anything Else that I can think of.

The ineffable poetry of existence is being destroyed by the cheap edition. Most mortals nowadays (with the happy exception of myself) are the victims of common sense.

Common sense is the patchouli of life: it destroys the aromatic fragrance of romance. Alas! that Boccaccio now is but a synonym for "Booksellers' Row."

Surely there is a fragile beauty about a dainty volume of verse: its form is so slender, its circulation so small. Is it possible to define beauty? The sage says, "No." Therefore let us attempt it.

Beauty is the jam upon the bread of life.
Life is the jam upon the bread of beauty.
Jam is the beauty upon the life of bread.

Which way will you have it? The epigram is equally profound each way. Happy is the man who has a quiver full of patent reversible aphorisms!

What a glorious death it would be to die of a surfeit of books!—a far nobler ideal than that of the Persian poet Lhywis Carolwan, who warbled for

"Buns and buns and buns."

Books—those nebulous neighings of neurotic ninnies, those yellow rhodomontades full of sound and fury signifying revolutions, those mellifluous rose-bubbles sung in the Lane of Bodley and echoed by the murmuring Logs of Rolen.

There is beauty in the extracts of all essences, did we but look for it. There is Beauty in the Bellow of the Blast, as my favourite Japanese poetess, Katisha, has often observed.

Even Religion is beautiful—but I have given that a pretty booklet to itself.

A book should be pleasing to the eye and satisfying to the ear. Give us a dainty cover and a cool, creamy margin; but the print—oh, the pity o't!—it looks so straight, so formal, so black. Why have any print? Why anything to sully the pure, undulating depths of uncut edges? Let us, like Nature, be careless of the type. Thrice happy day when, in opening some dainty dream of binding, the eye shall fall lovingly on the beauty of blank pages.

On Myself.

Some brother poet has remarked that "we rise on stepping-stones . . . to higher things." The middle portion of this observation I have omitted owing to its irrelevance.

Irrelevance is, none the less, a charming thing, for on these few graceful irrelevancies—the stepping-stones of Spring and Books—have I risen to higher things in the shape of myself.

But having attained to that egotistic peak in Darien, there is no reason why I should be silent, and rather would I leave to others "the wild surmise."

May I confess to a weakness? Let me

whisper it gently for fear the soft, long-eared quadruped should murmur it in his love trills to the albine, slim-necked bird—not echo of classic fame, but rather *anser*. My heart is bound in limited edition cords to the maiden Levia. True, I have flirted occasionally with Nobilia, but indeed it was but a passing amour committed in the hot haste of youth and purple cloth. And it has always been my aim to bear in mind the advice of the Latin poet Nemo, which I have freely translated thus:—

"Be trivial, Poet : let who will be serious
Pen dainty *mots;* be neat and never long,
Thus making problems wherewith sages weary us
A sweet meat song!"

FANTASIE.

CINQUANTE ANS APRÈS.

(Dedicated to the shade of Alexandre Dumas, author of "Trois Mousquetaires." "Vin'gt Ans Après," &c.)

CHAPTER I.

INTRODUCING THE HERO.

THE town of Abbeville was in a state of intense political excitement.

Uproarious were the party cries.

Along the high-road galloped a young man, mounted on a noble steed. This young man wore a sage-green cloak—the colour being suggestive in more ways than one. It was green—that denoted his youth; it was sage—that denoted his wisdom. Yes; though but nineteen, he possessed the sagacity of a man three times his age, and he had an intuitive knowledge of human affairs which would have put mighty Richelieu in the background. Yet, alas! he lacked one thing, for which even genius will not compensate.

That thing was money. Gaston Merivale de Paraphine was a poor man.

He cogitated on his hard lot as he rode along, and gave a deep sigh, which encouraged a lame man to importune him for alms.

"*Au Diable!*" cried the well-bred and idiomatic youth.

Two men whom he met laughed as they passed him. The bare idea that he had, perhaps, a smut on his nose incensed our hero beyond measure. With an ominous contraction of his finely-cut lips, he circled the glistening steel, and the next moment one man rolled a headless corpse on the ground; then, with his left hand, he dealt the comrade a reeling blow which killed him instantaneously.

The young man smiled scornfully; he was naturally kind-hearted, but the proud blood of the Paraphines flowed in his veins. He dug the spurs into his steed and was soon lost to sight.

The Commissaire of the Police had watched the scene from his bedroom window. He was narrow-minded, and could not understand the exuberant spirits of youth; and whilst you, reader, no doubt sympathise with the bold spirit of our hero, the cold-blooded Commissaire was preparing a warrant.

CHAPTER II.

CONTAINING ANOTHER ADVENTURE OF THE HERO.

The inn at Perigord, known as "Le Cochon et le Sifflet," was renowned for its good fare. Travellers rarely passed it by.

At sunset, on a certain day subsequent to the events recounted in the previous chapter, a horseman came galloping up, dismounted, and, after brief directions about his steed, entered the inn.

The host advanced for orders.

"I wish for a dinner, and that right sharply," said the stranger, with that delicate courtesy which is inbred in some natures.

"Yes, monsieur."

"Wine good?"

"The best in France, monsieur."

The youth (who is our hero, as the reader may have surmised from the refinement of his speech) glanced round him distrustfully.

"Has a stranger in a large, sky-blue hat been here?" he murmured, in hoarse tones.

"Oh no, monsieur."

"Good. Bring up two dozen of your choicest Bordeaux, and, stop!—a fat capon."

The host bowed profoundly and departed.

The evening crept on, and Gaston, with the healthy flush of youth on his cheeks, was just completing his fifteenth bottle. Suddenly a sound of horse's hoofs was heard, and a tall, powerfully-built man entered, wearing an enormous, sky-blue, felt hat, which, being decidedly too large for him, concealed the upper part of his face. Gaston leapt to his feet, a fierce wave of passion traversing the classic serenity of his aristocratic countenance. "Villain!" he cried. "Draw instantly, or, *morbleu!* you are a dead man."

A scornful light burnt in one of the stranger's eyes, his hat being pulled down over the other.

"Host," said he, in deep, rich tones, "we depute you to be seconds, doctor, and witness."

The host evinced great distress, and, catching his feet at the same instant against some empty bottles, he fell down with a resounding smack and evinced even more distress. The sound of clashing steel was heard for a few minutes; then suddenly, Gaston transfixed the blue hat of his opponent.

Both stepped back in utter astonishment.

"Parbleu! The friend of my childhood," ejaculated the youth; "Vicomte Bombominet."

"Gaston! The only son of my dearest friend," murmured the other, in tones husky with emotion.

"But where did you get that hat?" said our hero, with sudden suspicion.

"I will tell you. It formerly belonged to my neighbour. On meeting him one day I asked him whether he was in the 'blues.' He answered not a word. I resented the insult and challenged him. He took no heed. Enraged beyond measure I slew him, and wear his hat as a trophy."

"My noble friend!" said the youth, with fervour. "'Twas the Duc de Popocatapetl, the enemy of our house and kindred, who is stone deaf."

The friends embraced affectionately; even the innkeeper found difficulty in preserving an impassive countenance.

"Some wine," demanded Bombominet, "and let it be the best you have!"

"What was the mystery of my father's life, and how was he indebted to you?" inquired Gaston, when the wine appeared.

Bombominet first drank off three bottles in succession, then cleared his throat, and said, "It is a long story, but one that you should hear. Your father from an early age evinced a tender-hearted disposition, allied with sound business instinct. When but a child, a pedlar came one day to the house with wares; your father immediately brought down his dinner ('twas a *chaud-froid de mouton*), and gave it to the poor man; then, while the latter was thanking him, he secretly purloined two of the best pocket-knives from the pedlar's goods. It was not surprising, therefore, that at the age of sixteen he fell in love with a charming actress of thirty-two, who had amassed a considerable fortune. On both sides the parents were obdurate. He resolved to carry her off. One evening he received a note intimating that his great uncle had expired, and had left his fortune to him. He immediately resolved to comply with his parents' wishes, and to marry as they desired. He was hastening to tell them so when an aged man accosted him. 'Be not rash,' he said, 'letters may lie; but not so the third cousin of your grandmother's youngest nephew, who bids you——'"

A snore interrupted Bombominet; he looked for his companion, but beheld him not; he looked under the table; there lay Gaston in profound slumber, embracing an empty bottle.

A weird smile illumined the stranger's countenance; he softly withdrew, after finishing what was left of the wine.

CHAPTER III.

NEMESIS.

Our hero awoke the next morning with a racking headache, to find himself recumbent on the floor, and affectionately embracing a bottle. He smiled feebly: "Bombominet—early walk—s'pose," he murmured, as he brushed a wandering beetle off his face.

"Well," he thought, as he sat down on the

nearest chair, "I wonder how the charming Léonie is this morning, likewise the adorable Thérèse and the saucy Filette." He opened his pocket-book, and drew forth three *billets doux* which he lovingly regarded; "and these," he thought, "are from Madame Le Bœuf, my butcher's wife, Préfet Justin's mother-in-law, Madame Vinègre, and the last from my excellent bootmaker's aunt, a sweet woman though somewhat advanced in years." These ruminations were suddenly disturbed by mine host with a bill.

"One hundred and twenty-five francs!" muttered the young man, as he nervously felt in his pockets, but only brought to light his pocket-book, a sombre-looking handkerchief, twenty large brass buttons, and a purse containing a few sous.

A thought struck him. "Bring my horse round!" he said; and he secretly filled the purse with buttons.

He dropped the purse with a princely air into the innkeeper's hands, as he mounted his horse and rode off.

"One of the old nobility," muttered the man, his eyes glistening with greedy satisfaction.

"A thieving adventurer!" he exclaimed, when he noted the contents.

At this moment the Commissaire of the Police and some followers appeared.

"Quick! you will catch him—he is on the high-road to Marseilles," howled the enraged host, anticipating their inquiries.

"Onward!" called the Commissaire to his men.

Meanwhile our hero, who had almost forgotten the recent incident, was riding leisurely, when, on looking back, he noticed horseman rapidly advancing.

They were covering him on every side, leaving no room for escape; so murmuring, " A Paraphine never runs away," he checked his steed and awaited them with drawn sword.

"Consider yourself under arrest," said the Commissaire as he came up, with as much sternness as was possible, considering he was out of breath.

"*Parbleu!* and why?"

The Commissaire motioned to a dark, silent figure beside him. "Will you explain?" he said.

"Young man," began the stranger, with a

gloomy smile, "I represent the reading public so allow me to inform you that you are no longer popular."

Gaston grew pale with horror.

"The modern reader," continued the stranger, "cares not to have his imagination harassed with impossible escapades and incredible feats. His soul revolts from the monotonous success of a dissipated hero. His common sense will not perplex itself with the triumph of vice through one hundred and ninety-nine pages, and virtue's victory on the two hundredth."

"No! the modern hero must be something more than a braggart *roué*. To be acceptable to the reading public he must now pass through at least six phases of religious belief."

"Alas! I never passed through one," murmured Gaston.

"He must expound social theories," resumed the other, "the more heterodox the better. He must quote from Henry George, and should be well up in the various doctrines of Lassalle and Karl Marx.

"Dialectics, moreover, are preferable to duels; and the villain need not be a duke, but should be an Evangelical Dissenter, in order that he may have long arguments with the hero when in his agnostic phase.

"The conversations need not show profound thought, but must be smart and plausible——"

"Stop!" cried Gaston, "I can bear no more; am I no longer liked and admired?"

"No, you are out of date completely," said the stranger, with cruel distinctness.

Gaston Merivale de Paraphine fell from his horse and expired without a groan.

A CHRISTMAS MIXTURE.

(One teaspoonful taken twice a day after meals will ensure a sound and refreshing sleep.)

THE annual dinner of the "Royal Society of Pot-Boilers" was drawing to a conclusion. All the best anecdotes had been told. The speeches were over, in which everybody had proposed everybody else's health, and eternal friendships had been sworn between men not generally on speaking terms. Perhaps the Max Sutaine and '51 port had something to do with this. Then some one proposed story-telling, and the idea caught on.

A comic journalist who had had a complimentary ticket, suggested telling the truth for a change, but this witticism was received coldly, and he retired abashed behind his filberts.

The Chairman called on the Realistic writer

to start. The Realist was in fine form, being unusually dyspeptic.

"Christmas Eve was close and humid. Outside, a thick, sulphurous, fog wrapt everything in its foul embrace. Inside, the gas-vitiated atmosphere reduced Silas Moody to a state of inertia and violent headache.

"He was sitting in a springless armchair, cogitating over the past. A cricket hopped gloomily towards the fireless grate. 'Poor insect,' hissed Silas, with bitter scorn, 'wouldst live in a world like this? Nay, foolish one, seek Nirvana, since there is no sentimental Dickens now to accord thee undue importance' —and he crushed it with his foot.

"The discordant sound of cracked church bells broke on the suffering air. Silas looked out of his garret window, and through a gap in the fog saw a dust-cart passing. 'Such is life,' said he, fixing his eyes on the cobwebs in the corner of the room. 'Little more than a mound of refuse. In it, a few lucky wights find jewels, more find bits of glass; most find only ashes and filth—and what thinks she who lives with me?'

"Here the leg of the chair came off, and he

continued his soliloquy on the floor. 'The world is a sewer———'"

"Time, time," interposed the Chairman, hastily. "Would Mr. Buttercups now oblige?"

Mr. Buttercups not only would but did. He was a regular contributor to the "Family Slops" and the "Infant's Drivel."

"'Yes,' repeated Silas, 'the world is as sure' (an inarticulate protest from the Realist) 'to prove a mine of blessing, a fountain of joy, a land of plenty, an ocean of bliss, as———'"

"'As the twentieth volume of the "Family Slops,"'" said his unmarried sister, who entered at that moment, and brought down some of the plaster from the ceiling with her ponderous tread. Silas smiled joyfully. 'Sweet little Sis,' he said, 'it shall cheer me with its radiance,' and putting it into the grate he applied a match.

"'Listen, Silly,' said little Sis, 'listen to the message of the bells.' And she opened the window letting in ('the fog,' snarled the Realist under his breath) 'the joyful sound,' which seemed to speak of the delights of a didactic sister, who would read to him in silvern tones some of Longfellow's worst poems when he was lying on a bed of pain, bringing back a flood of recollections——"

A loud snore from the Chairman interrupted the eloquence of the Domestic writer. Then the Chairman suddenly awoke. "Shaving-water," he murmured—"I mean, Mr. Cupid kindly take up the bottle—that is to say—the thread of the story."

The Sentimental writer began in dulcet tones—

"In short, the bells reminded him that 'twas, indeed, Merry Yule Tide, and Silas, or, as his comrades jestingly dubbed him, Adonais, ran his slender fingers through his curly hair, passionately kissed a coloured miniature, and gazed dreamily at Gentle Luna, whose refulgent beams cast a subdued light on his classic profile—a profile which a cloistered monk——"

At this point Mr. Cupid stopped for breath, and Mr. Curdler took advantage of the fact to continue with the story.

"Even such a monk as he, whose dusky portrait glaring at him through the gloom, might have envied. Suddenly the sister shrieked, 'Hist, brother! has not the clock struck twenty-nine? Something is wrong.'

Subsequent events justified her words. The floor gave a mighty crack, and she disappeared from view. The fire burnt blue. Silas felt his hair rising; he rose also. There was a clanking of chains, and a phosphorescent gleam, which played over the cupboard where the cheese was kept. 'Silas,' said a weird and sinister-looking being, 'cease to think of her you love—I, a ghost, love her, and mean to keep her for myself. Nay, think not to flee, two escaped maniacs are in the drawing-room, another rival is outside the door with a revolver, and a couple of bloodthirsty uncles are coming down the chimney armed with bowie-knives.'"

"Thank you," said the Chairman, politely, "but some of us have some way to walk before we reach home to-night. Now, Mr. Morbid, just a little from you." The psychologico-physiologico-pathological writer went on—

"'Pish,' said Silas, to the phantom, 'what are you but a diseased condition of the sensory nerve ganglia reacting on the visual organs, and giving rise to distinct subjective sensations? But you will find it all in any elementary physiology.' Then he put on his hat, went out, and picked a person's pocket. A few minutes later he was explaining with compassionate indulgence to a policeman that he was but an automaton—the victim of hereditary impulse.

"'My great-grandfather,' he observed, 'had a violent temper, which has reappeared in me!' Here he knocked the policeman down, stamped on him, and quietly resumed his way.

"'No,' said Neuronica to him, an hour later, 'you are a poor creature, and I do not love you; but I cannot help it, being a consistent determinist. Yet I admit you are an interesting study, so I will marry you.'

"'Be it so,' replied Silas. 'After all, what is love? Analyse it—consider it from the sickliest standpoint, and it is but the glorification——'"

"Please don't encroach on the lady novelist's domain," put in the Chairman, firmly. "And now, gentlemen, perhaps we had better stop."

Then he gazed sternly at the comic journalist who had taken advantage of the story to finish up the rest of the port.

THE NEW CINDERELLA.

AN UP-TO-DATE FAIRY TALE.

CINDERELLA sat disconsolately by her boudoir fire. She was very unhappy, and felt a great desire to sob. But she sternly repressed this feeling, conscious that tear-stained cheeks were unbecoming, and mindful of the fact that a violent expression of emotion in private was so much wasteful expenditure of nervous force. True, her external surroundings suggested every possible comfort and luxury. She had an indulgent father, who made her a handsome allowance, and slept resignedly during her mandoline performances, and a self-sacrificing mother, who ruined her nerves chaperoning her girls during the London season. But affectionate parents are a drug in the market, and

THE NEW CINDERELLA. 63

Cinderella felt that mere affection and indulgence from parents grows painfully monotonous after a time. She yearned for something more ; her mind was in a ferment of unrest and dissatisfaction, for had she not just thrown aside her latest craze, and there was nothing to take its place? Bitterly she mused over past and defunct fads, as she sipped her morning chocolate (an institution she had borrowed from an old French novel), and since there was still half an hour before her mandoline master came, she had ample time for indulging in the luxury of grief.

How well she remembered ('twas one long year since), when on returning from a Parisian finishing school she had taken up private theatricals, with such enthusiasm as a "finished" young lady deemed it decorous to show. She had commenced, of course, with easy parts, such as *Juliet* and *Lady Macbeth;* and after studying simple *rôles* like these, she had aspired to "higher things," which meant in her case subtle and complicated psychological studies, provided by some friend suffering from Ibsomania. Her absurdly conventional parents protested against this transition from the "legitimate" to the illegitimate drama, and the poor girl had to relinquish second-rate psychology for skirt-dancing.

Soon, however, this craze expired, and another reigned in its stead. She went in for philanthropic dabbling; recited unsuitable poems at East End teas; talked about "elevating the masses" (as if she had been a kind of steam crane); took umbrage because she fancied Mr. Du Maurier caricatured her, and gave up *Punch* and Philanthropy in disgust.

And then the futility and barrenness of her existence appealed to her. She read in one of the monthlies an article on Pessimism, which enabled her to talk authoritatively about the utter worthlessness of life. She poured out her soul nightly in a strictly private and confidential diary, expressed her sentiments in violet ink, and complained that she was conscious of a baulked personality.

After a time this grew monotonous, and now for the first time she envied her elder sisters, who had only experienced one craze apiece, but had stuck to it. Better be Secretary to the Emancipated Women's Social and Political Reformation League, like Priscilla, or write turgid prose full of asterisks and hysterics, like Isabel, than be absolutely crazeless!

"Anything I can do for you in the way of crazes?" said a voice.

Cinderella looked up, and saw her fairy godmother standing beside her, though she had substituted for the conventional cone hat the latest fashion in bonnets, and carried a parasol for a wand, since even a fairy should not be behind the times.

"La vie est vaine," sighed Cinderella.

"You've got it badly, I am afraid," said the fairy, reflectively; "but I know what you want: you wish to rise above the petty trammels of sex; to have scope for developing your individuality; to escape from the paralysing monotony of home-life: here is the grand secret—you must write a novel!"

"I never could," began Cinderella.

"I never said you *could*," interposed the other, sharply; "I said you *must*. If only people who could write novels did so, what do you think would become of the circulating libraries?"

Cinderella felt unable to cope with this poser. "Well," she said, "I can try. Father has one or two translations of German Rationalistic Theology. If I read those, I suppose I shall be qualified?"

"Certainly not," replied the fairy, contemptuously. "The popularity of the theological novel is on the wane. Mudie's patrons are growing tired of weak-kneed clergymen and agnostic moral giants. They have been fed so long on religious doubts that they want a change of mental diet, for they have positively no room for one doubt more. No, the youthful hero who once spoke so touchingly about pretty religious myths, and who quoted Strauss, Baur and Renan in *tête-à-tête* with his *fiancée* must now garnish his small talk with extracts from Griesinger, Ribot, and Maudsley."

The fairy tapped Cinderella's writing-table with her parasol, and a small parcel of books lay on the table. "Here are 'Diseases of the Brain,' by Forbes Winslow, Quain's 'Medical Dictionary,' and a treastise on 'Heredity.' With these your literary outfit is complete. Imbue your mind with every grade of mental pathology, and the product will be a sickly exotic of first-class morbidness. Appear to sneer at all your characters—which may not be so difficult as you imagine. Style is immaterial, provided it glitters with inversions of the commonplace — called by some, epigrams. And now, my dear, good-bye."

"Stop a minute," said Cinderella; "I have some verses which nearly every editor and publisher has refused. Can I make no use of them?"

"Oh yes," said the fairy, drily, "there is always a last resource for rejected poets." She waved her parasol, and in a twinkling fifty large-paper copies, duly signed and numbered, appeared instead of the soiled MSS.

Cinderella almost clapped her hands. Luckily, she recalled herself in time, before committing such a barbarity. "Now I shall become talked about and paragraphed, and even my depressions will be a pleasure when I can confide them to interviewers."

"Yes, you will be quite the rage for a time."

"And become quite famous, shall I not?"

"Well, that's another story," said the fairy, with a smile. "But I must say good-bye, since other Cinderellas await me."

"HOW TO BE A DRAMATIC CRITIC."

An Imaginary Scene.

I WAS borne along, with the crowd of eager young journalists, to the New Dramatic Institute, which had been recently opened. Large posters outside the building advertised a series of short lectures for 3 p.m., on "How to be a Dramatic Critic"; but, owing to the number of men bent on the same errand as myself, I was able to make my way but slowly.

We passed by numerous lecture-rooms, in one of which a gentleman, whose name was either Jones, Brown, or Robinson, was holding forth on the "Inferiority of Religion to the Drama as a moral educator for the people";

"HOW TO BE A DRAMATIC CRITIC." 69

whilst on the doors of another room I noticed a placard stating that a university professor was lecturing on the "Advantages of a Classical Education for writing opera-bouffe and burlesques."

A programme was thrust into my hands as I pressed into the lecture-hall, and on glancing at it I found that two well-known critics were going to expound their views on the subject of dramatic criticism, and that various minor lights would also speak on the subject.

The first was already about to speak as a representative of the Impressionist School.

He told us that we were at all costs to be artistic; that violent abuse was a sign of *bourgeoisie*, of an uncultured mind. The business of the critic, he said, was to enjoy as much as was possible; when he could not enjoy, let him delicately insinuate that he was bored, [metaphorically], shrug his shoulders, and pass on to a more agreeable topic. Let him taste the various dramatic dishes, and report to the public how they affected his palate.

This lecturer concluded his remarks by chalking up on a blackboard a specimen of "Impressionistic" criticism, hypothetically assuming that Mr. Irving had produced a play of Shakspeare's.

"What was it like? How did it affect me? Well, let me think. I have a pleasant remembrance of green, swaying boughs and charming rural scenery, grimly frowning battlements and the hoarse cries of a rude soldiery. The most delightful harmony of colours in Act 3 proved most grateful to the eyes, and I could almost have imagined that I was in some sequestered glade in the South of England, had I not been forcibly reminded that I was in the Strand, by the extreme narrowness of my stall. (Mr. Irving, by the by, ought really to give us more commodious stalls—say like those at the Empire.)

"I confess frankly that I did not enjoy Act 4. Yes, I know the acting was fine, but one of the peasants had a spot on his nose, which appeared to increase in size each time he said, 'A right good welcome, my liege'; this was irritating.

"A great deal of admiration has been expended on the magnificent interior in Act 1. It may be bad taste, but I positively disliked it. It reminded me of an old painting which

"HOW TO BE A DRAMATIC CRITIC." 71

used to hang up in my grandmother's drawing-room, just over the corner in which I (often, alas!) stood for punishment. And the acting. That on the whole was supremely satisfying. Miss Terry, with her sweet, kittenish movements and picturesque draperies, was a treat to watch and listen to. As for Mr. Irving, there is always a *soupçon* of *diablerie* about anything he undertakes. Can I describe my feelings when he first came on? As a certain character in one of Molière's masterpieces says, 'C'est impossible!' I have seen Mr. A. throw more tragic intensity into the part; I have seen Monsieur B. display greater emotional power, and Signor C. portray finer intellectual subtlety. But Mr. Irving played it as only Mr. Irving can, &c., &c."

The Impressionist advocate now gave place to a representative of the Analytical and Hypercritical School.

I was unable to catch all his earlier remarks, but from what I did hear he appeared to be deploring the fact that there was no modern English play worthy of serious criticism, and he warned would-be critics that they must look abroad—say to Scandinavia—did they wish to find any drama worthy of the critic's art.

As for style, he recommended a confident and dogmatic tone, free from flippancy, and chary in praise. He concluded, like the previous lecturer, with a sample on the blackboard, which he assured us would, with very few alterations and additions, do for any Shakspearean revival at the "Lyceum."

"I commend Mr. Irving for choosing this play by the Elizabethan dramatist, because, although one of the worst acting plays conceivable, it is, nevertheless, a fine piece of literature. I quite admit that Shakspeare was much, if not altogether, indebted to a German romance current about 1560, for the story of the play, nevertheless . . . (here supply various historical details interspersed with learned remarks about the 'quarto' and 'folio') . . . I regret that I must dissent from my friend Mr. X., and, in fact, from all other critics, as to the value of Mr. Irving's interpretation of the principal *rôle*.

"To have succeeded, he ought, I take it, to strike at first a subdued note, then rise to Act 4 in a gradual crescendo of passion. The famous

"HOW TO BE A DRAMATIC CRITIC." 73

soliloquy (or soliloquies, as the case may be), should be delivered free from rant, yet with strong emotional force, flavoured with a suggestion of intellectual reserve.

"His acting at the beginning of the Act should be in the spirit of genuine melodrama; in the middle, that of pure comedy; at the end, emphatically that of pure and simple tragedy. But Mr. Irving does not realise this conception at all, &c."

This gentleman was followed by various others, each advocating different principles and formulating diverse rules.

The advocate of ordinary descriptive journalese advised us to give as much attention to the audience as to the piece; to note the various celebrities present, and watch when they laughed and applauded. As for the acting, it was always safe to say that "Miss Terry was the personification of womanly grace," that Mr. A. acted in his "usual vigorous style," and that Miss B. "won golden opinions."

There was something at once familiar and strange about these remarks and samples. As I wended my way out of the Institute, I racked my brain to discover where and when I had seen or heard something very like this, and whilst I cogitated—

. . . . .

I awoke, and behold, it was a dream!

THE GAME OF INTERVIEWING.

(With rules and full directions.)

THIS amusing and instructive game may be learned in a very short time, and will prove a diverting pastime in long winter evenings.

Only two people are required—the interviewer and the interviewee: of these the former is the more important. Any child may learn this game, provided his father can fight: for unlimited cheek and a fertile imagination are the only requisites. The latter especially will be found useful, should the notes of the interview get lost before publication. There are two things to be kept in view when playing this game: (1) Always question the interviewee on matters with which he is not conversant; (2)

Never neglect the conversational machine (given gratis), which will expand the most barren interview into one, two, or three columns, as required.

Appended are various examples :—

1.—THE LITERARY INTERVIEW.

(A chat with Mr. Blank, the celebrated Novelist and Poet.)

Directly I entered the portal of Gimcrack Villa I felt that there was a distinct literary air about the place—a kind of cultured draughtiness as it were.

I awaited the arrival of Mr. B. in the charming little drawing-room. By the fire sat a favourite cat with a Sterne-like smile upon its countenance, and there was a parrot by the window which, by his observations, I conjectured to be a student of Fielding.

"You look harassed, Mr. B.," I remarked, after we had cordially shaken hands. "You are suffering from mental strain, consequent ——"

"No," he said, with a deprecating smile.

"True, my work is arduous, but—well—the—fact is my daughter is learning cookery; we had experiments for lunch to-day."

I nodded feelingly, and was seized with sympathetic dyspepsia.

After a moment's painful silence I inquired, "Now as to your last novel, concerning which so many eulogistic reviews——"

"I never read reviews of my own books," he interposed, quickly, adding *sotto voce*, "I get other people to read them to me. True," he continued, slowly closing one eye (a peculiar habit of his, and particularly characteristic of talented men), "I hear casually that I am compared to Scott, Dickens, Thackeray, Balzac, Hugo, Pope, and, of course," with a gentle smile, "I have been hailed as another Tennyson, a new Browning. I do not think much of these terms. I cannot tell you," he added, earnestly, "how pained I am when I hear friends say that I remind them of Shakspeare or Goëthe."

I admitted that it must be very painful.

"Be original, is my motto," said Mr. B., with enthusiasm, knocking down a cheap vase and kicking the cat accidentally. "Educate the public taste with your literary wares and you will provide food for them that will be fit for ——"

"Cat's-meat," interjected the parrot, inappropriately, with an eye fixed on pussy's tail.

Mr. B. laughed, though not heartily. Fearing he was growing tired, I changed the subject. "Is it true you dislike gooseberry jam?"

"Absolutely false," repudiated the litterateur, with vehemence, "please contradict it. Now had the rumour been about raspberry jam I would have admitted the truth——" he hesitated.

"Powders when a boy?" said I.

He nodded.

The ornamental clock on the mantlepiece, the hands of which pointed to one o'clock, here struck seventeen, so I concluded it was time for me to depart. And, as Artemus Ward would say, "I wented." (If you desire to use the serious stop, and not the comic, in the conversational machine, you can conclude: "And thus mentally braced up by my chat with this invigorating thinker I departed, and leaving the cosy room, the home of the Muses, plunged into the atmosphere of the London streets.")

2.—THE PARADOXICAL INTERVIEW.

(N.B.—This variation is very rare and extremely trying. It must be used with caution.)

"May I have a few minutes with you, Mr. Glitter?"

Mr. Glitter was emerging from a confectioner's, and he flicked the crumbs off his mouth with an old-fashioned grace.

"A bun," he remarked, opening a cigarette-case inlaid with rubies, and producing a cigarette veritably gold-tipped. "A bun is the uneatable designed——"

"Please tell me about yourself," I asked, humbly (hoping to lead him away from the epigrams so familiar to the public).

"Myself," said the great man, dreamily watching the blue smoke curling from the cigarette. "I should talk on, on, for ever. This personality" (with an artistic flourish towards himself) "is an inexhaustible topic of converse; a theme rich in suggestiveness; a spring of undying originality—but, shall I waste it?"

I clutched my umbrella timidly.

"You, you—a journalist?" He regarded me

with bitter scorn. Then shortly and distinctly, "I *loathe* journalists and wasps, dramatic critics and black beetles—in fact, everything but myself."

I opened my umbrella for protection, but he became abstracted, so I closed it again.

"The public admire you," I said, almost in a whisper, fearing another outbreak.

"The toad likes the sun," said Mr. G. "Does it follow that the sun likes the toad? If the toad likes the warmth of the sun, is it not natural?"

He threw the end of his cigarette away and resumed—(here I felt so unwell in my mental efforts to elucidate his meaning that I became oblivious to what followed).

A slight turn of the conversational machine will make the interview up to the requisite column.

3.—THE THEATRICAL INTERVIEW· (FEMALE).

(N.B.—If the interviewee is ugly, refer to her as interesting ; if plain, speak of her as charming and attractive ; if pretty—consult the dictionary for adjectives.)

"Tea?" said Miss Frolic, with a charming smile.

THE GAME OF INTERVIEWING.

"Thank you—one lump, please—thanks, very much."

"And do you like the stage, do you——"

"Oh, please not so quick." She threw back her head with a dainty movement. "Of course one likes to feel one has magnetised one's audience; one" (Miss Frolic modestly avoided the obstructive ego) "likes to feel the audience are, so to speak, in one's power; yes, I suppose my song 'Oops-a-diddle, dum-do' is a success."

"Overwhelming," was my enthusiastic reply.

"Not that I only care for the stage," she put in, with pretty eagerness. "No, I am training pet snails to turn somersaults. Then I dote on books——"

"Ah," I said, interested, "please tell me your opinion on the disadvantages of a complex civilisation!"

But we will stop our samples here, since enough have been given to show the fascinating character of this ingenious game.

THROUGH THE (POLITICAL) LOOKING-GLASS, AND WHAT ALICE SAW THERE.

A Retrospective Fragment.

DRAMATIS PERSONÆ.

WHITE KING . .	*Lord Rosebery.*
WHITE QUEEN . .	*Sir William Harcourt.*
A WHITE PAWN . .	*Mr. Campbell Bannerman*
TWEEDLEDUM } . .	*Rival Candidates.*
TWEEDLEDEE	

"THEY don't keep this house so tidy as the other," Alice thought to herself, as she noticed several members with their hats over their eyes, and their legs sprawling all about the place.

Here something began squeaking on the front fender, and made Alice turn her head in time to see a White Pawn replying to some questions that had been put to him. Alice watched curiously to see what would happen next.

"It is the voice of my child!" the White Queen cried out, as she rushed into the lobby.

A bell rang somewhere, and after the tumult had subsided Alice noticed that the White King, who had just hurried up from Durdans, was knocked over.

"My precious Bannerman! my expert Secretary!" cried the White Queen, wringing her hands.

The King was sulky. He had been hurt—not to say surprised—by the fall, and felt entitled to be a little annoyed. He murmured a few lines from Longfellow's poem on "Resignation" to himself.

When the Queen had recovered herself a little she called out to the White King, "Mind public opinion!"

"What public opinion?" said the King, looking anxiously toward Epsom, as if he thought that was the most likely place to find it.

"Look out for the General Election," panted the Queen; "mind the Unionists do not get in."

They then consulted together in frightened whispers.

"The horror of this crisis," remarked the King, "I shall never forget!"

"You will, though," the Queen said, "if you happen to get into power again."

Alice looked on with interest as the King took out a note-book and began writing. A sudden thought struck her, and she took hold of the end of the pencil and began writing for him.

The poor King looked puzzled and unhappy, and at last he panted out, "I can't manage this pencil a bit; it writes all manner of things I don't intend."

"What manner of things?" said the Queen, looking over the book (in which Alice had put "Sir Visto won the last Derby, Sir Veto will lose the next one"). "I hope that's not a memorandum of your feelings."

There was a book lying near by, and while she sat watching the White King Alice turned over the leaves to find some part that she could read, "for it's all in some strange language I don't know," she said to herself. Then a bright thought struck her. "Why, it's a canvassing book!" she exclaimed; "and here are some verses called 'The Jabberrotter, a warning to the borough voter at Election time.'"

This is what she read—

"'Twas Julig, and the canvas droves
 Did gas and quibble in the street;
All heckly were the borough coves,
 The candidates discreet.

'Beware the Jabberrot, my son!
 The words of rant, the phrases catch!
Beware the pot-house bribe, and shun
 The vagrant voter snatch!'

And as in muddled thought he stood,
 The Jabberrot of canvas fame,
Came purely for the voters' good,
 And piffled when he came!

'It is not true. What, vote for you!
 Who wants to see your party back?'
The voter said; the monster fled
 And tried another tack.

'And hast thou snubbed the Jabberrot?
 Crow not so fast, my simple boy!
See others come! a few, a lot!
 And smile with fearful joy.'

'Twas Julig, and the canvas droves
 Did gas and quibble in the street;
All whimsy were the borough coves,
 The candidates discreet."

"It seems very exciting," said Alice, when she had finished it, "but it is rather hard to understand! However, there's a contest *somewhere* about *something*—that's clear, at any rate."

．　　　．　　　．　　　．　　　．

Suddenly Alice became aware of two huge posters, one underneath the other. One was marked "Vote for Tweedledum, and free tea and treacle all the year round." The other was marked, "Vote for Tweedledee, and twopenny twists of tobacco every other Thursday."

"They both seem very generous," said Alice; "I'll just go and see what they are like."

They were standing on opposite sides of the road, shaking their fists at one another.

"If you think we're not friendly you're mistaken," said Tweedledum. "Our animosity is purely political, quibbler!"

"Word Juggler!" responded the other, warmly. "You're quite right—apart from an inherent political dishonesty and intellectual meanness, I've the greatest respect for you."

(Then both together.) "We're going to pursue this contest without any personalities whatever. The personal element (contrary to all other similar contests) will be quite eliminated."

Here they both shook hands watchfully, and without enthusiasm.

"I don't know what you're thinking about," said Tweedledum, "but I'm in favour of it, decidedly."

"So am I," said Tweedledee, "so don't let that prevent you from voting for me."

"I haven't got a vote," remarked Alice.

"More she has," said Dum and Dee, gazing blankly at each other. "Then why are you taking up our valuable time? Do you suppose any human being without a vote can interest a candidate?"

"Don't irritate her," whispered Dee, "she may have a vote some day." (Then aloud) "Let me repeat you a poem."

"Is it political?" asked Alice, doubtfully.

"Well—yes—in a sort of way," said Dee, with a smile. "But if you want to ask any question, hand it up to the chairman, and it shall be answered in due course after the resolution in favour of my candidature has been carried."

"It's poor stuff," remarked Dum, with a

superior smile, " but you'd better listen to it ; it will show to what depths of doggerel and abysses of inanity political verse can descend."

Tweedledee murmured something about the law of libel, and then consulted the " Corrupt Practices Act" to see whether he might pull the other's nose. Obtaining no information on this point, he pulled it metaphorically, and commenced—

> "The Premier and Radical
>   Were standing side by side.
> 'We two,' remarked the Radical,
>   ' Can never be allied.'
> And this was odd, because, you know,
>   They subsequently tried.
>
> The Chancellor and Socialist
>   Were walking close at hand ;
> The Fabian's Clarion voice denounced
>   The rich man holding land.
> ' If this were only nationalised,'
>   He said, ' it would be grand.'
>
> ' If Hardie (Keir) and Fabians
>   ' Ruled England for a year,
> ' Do you suppose,' the Fabian said,
>   ' Utopia would be here ?'
> ' I doubt it,' said the Chancellor
>   And taxed the bitter beer.

'The time has come,' the Premier said,
    ' To talk about arrears,
Of Local Veto, Church in Wales,
    ('Twill calm each section's fears),
And why Macgregor went away,
    And whether Lords are peers?'

' But wait a bit,' the Irish cried,
    ' You're really rather cool,
Pray what about your promises
    Relating to Home Rule?'
' No hurry,' said the Radical,
    ' I'm not a perfect fool.'

'To smash the Lords,' the Premier said,
    ' Is what we chiefly need ;
Home Rule and Disestablishment
    Are very good indeed.
Now, if you're clever, Irish, dear,
    You'll understand my lead.'

' I fear we don't,' the Irish cried,
    Turning a little blue ;
' After our Gladstone, it is sad
    To put our trust in you.'
' I've knighted Irving,' said the peer ;
    ' What more could Premier do?'

' It seems a shame,' the Premier said,
    ' To write me down a stick,
After my foreign policy,
    Which is the Hatfield trick.'
The Radical said nothing but
    ' The programme's spread too thick.'

'Electors,' cried the Premier,
'You see the work we've done;
Now put us into power again!'
But answer came there none—
And this was scarcely odd, because
The other side had won."[1]

---

[1] Most of the above verses appeared in the *Globe* for May 25, 1895.

AIRS.

THE MODERN YOUNG MAN TO HIS LOVE.

(Marlowe up to date.)

COME live with me and be my love,
And we will all the pleasures prove
That club and latchkey will provide,
Since such delight a modern bride.

Should I deny thee any boon,
Solicit then Sir Francis Jeune:
And if domestic duty palls,
O drown dull care in music-halls.

A risky novel shalt thou write,
Conventionality indict
With sentiments exceeding bold,
Where men are dross and women gold.

I grieve to ask thee, dearest Nan,
To wed "that odious creature—man":
Nor would I press the slavish ring,
But 'tis, I think, the usual thing.

Still, after all I've said to-day,
I cannot ask thee to obey :
So if these pleasures may thee move,
Then live with me and be my love!

SEASONABLE THOUGHTS.

(WRITTEN DURING THE HOT MAY TERM OF 1893.)

(With Apologies to the shade of R. B.)

O TO be in Cambridge,
Now that April's there!
And whoever wakes in Cambridge,
Wakens in a sultry glare,
Which makes one sigh for the primitive leaf;
Then, the flower-tout fills the lodger with grief,
For "any old bags, sir?"'s a bore you'll allow
In Cambridge now.

And after April when May follows,
And the Tripos man in the thick tome wallows
Mark how the crafty coach will spread his snare
To catch some desperate youth, once a gay rover,

Who dreams of lists, his name, alas! not there,
Then that fool Jones bawls all his songs twice
    over,
As if the tune he never could quite capture,
With his too careless rapture.
Yet, though Exams now darken many lives,
All will be gay when the " May week " arrives,
When pretty girls assert their pristine power,
Much nicer than this tedious lecture hour.

LOCKSLEY HALL.

(During Spring Cleaning.)

SISTERS, leave me here a little, till the cleaning out is done;
Leave me at my club, O mother, leave your noise-distracted son.

In the Spring domestic earthquakes banish every thought of rest;
In the Spring the busy housewife makes herself a daily pest.

In the Spring the annual cleaning—cleaning? Ah, well, there's the rub—
In the Spring the young man's fancy quickly turns to thoughts of club.

Many a morning waked I early with the burly workman's tread,
While I watched a scraggy hatstand looming darkly near my bed.

Many an evening was I greeted by the sickly
 smell of paint,
Found my father fuming frantic, and my sisters
 feeling faint.

O my mother's vernal madness! O my bedroom, mine no more!
O the dusty, dusty box-room! Better sleep
 upon the floor.

And I doubt that through the chaos any tidy
 purpose runs,
And the mother's heart is hardened to the protest of her sons.

Not in vain the lights of clubland. Forward,
 clubward let me range,
Let a hansom spin me thither, whilst I count
 my silver change.

PILLOW PHILOSOPHY.

("While the busy part of mankind are fast huddling on their clothes, are already up and about their occupation, content to have swallowed their sleep by wholesale, we choose to linger abed and digest our dreams . . . why should we get up?"
—*Essays of Elia*.)

O WISE Charles Lamb, philosopher profound!
To your immortal fame this will redound,
Who never on the tardy riser frowned
              Like other great Pots!
When the dull morning creeps in chill and gray,
Unwelcome promise of a dismal day,
Then bed becomes a blessing, as you say,
              Unlike sedate Watts.

Odi profanum—proverb-quoting herd,
Who prate about the (foolish) early bird;

Has it ne'er to these moralists occurred,
   The worm we ought to notice?
Contrariwise (as said great Tweedledee),
From its snug earthy bed, you will agree,
That it should rise, as late as late can be,
   A fact we ought to vote is.

Rise with the lark? why thus neglect my ease?
For fifty larks, I do not choose to freeze,
Larks keep no prosy lectures—wherefore, please,
   Should I so court chills?
Cease, maiden, thy tattooing on my door!
Let me digest my dreams, I ask no more,
Thus I—with just a *soupçon* of a snore
   Would lie. The thought thrills.

'Twixt sleep and waking, happy drowsy state,
When fortune smiles, who frowned so much of
 late,
When bills get paid, and duns no longer wait,
   My deeds ensuring blessing.
When plots for novels surge about the brain,
 Twould make my fortune did they but remain,
Alas! they vanish, I confess with pain
   Without enduring dressing.

How cold the air! I'll snug beneath the clothes,
Not in the least that I desire to doze,
But it would be—if from this couch I rose—
    A much repented leap!
Now, as for work to-day, I have a plan
Carefully schemed. First rise, well, if I can!
    (*A pause, taken up by yawns.*)
(True! Sancho Panza, "Blessed is—the—man
    That first invented Sleep.")

TO PICKWICK.

(A Dyspeptic Lament.)

OH, really, Mr. Pickwick, you've a wonderful digestion!
That you e'er have dyspeptic pangs I seriously question,
Not to mention Wardle's dinners take the famous shooting lunch,
When you drank so very freely of delicious cold milk punch;
How could you sleep it off so well! Pray make a slight suggestion?

Oh, Reverend Stiggins of the Ebenezer Chapel, come,
Confide what secret virtue lies in hot, pine-apple rum?
I find it very bilious, you drink from morn till night,

And barring one slight episode—appear to be all right,
Such drinking with long living should strike good abstainers dumb.

Then Smangles drinking deeply of cheap sherry in the morning,
And that convivial "Swarry" kept up till the day was dawning,
Old Weller's great capacity for (scarce diluted) brandy,
And even Mrs. Bardell with a bottle nice and handy;
Yet no one seems a whit the worse, or needs a doctor's warning.

I have no wish to criticise you in a vein satirical,
To comment on your ethics I have not thus become lyrical,
But the absolute impunity with which you gorge and guzzle,
I will confess, has always been to me a serious puzzle;
In short, each individual is a gastronomic miracle.

THE POETS AT SCHOOL.

(Suggested by Mr. Barry Pain's " Poets at Tea.")

SWINBURNE, who liked " tuck " :—

O Caramel, clinging and cloying,
O Peppermint, subtle and strong,
Can I, fitting language employing,
Sufficiently sound thee in song?

I love the crisp crunch and the crumble
Of Toffee, burned, burnished and brown ;
And for the fierce joy of the Jumble,
I trudge down each day to the town.

CALVERLEY, who found smoking didn't agree with him :—

You ask me why I shun the pipe,
And scorn the fragrant cigarette?
'Tis not because of age unripe
        As yet.

You scorn my callow youth and say
Smoke was not meant for one so green.
Please understand I am to-day
        Fourteen !

I could a tale unfold, 'tis true,
Though it is scarcely worth my while ;
And I feel very sure that you
        Would smile.

Since then my love for weed has waned
(In crises hair turns white, 'tis said ;
I only know that mine remained
        Quite red).

I care not for scholastic laws,
Await not the parental grant ;
I do not smoke (alack !) because
        I can't.

LONGFELLOW, who was fond of story-books :—

  Tell me oft in weekly numbers,
    Life is but a Haggard dream,
  Where the interest never slumbers,
    And the white man reigns supreme.

Life is grand beyond that portal
  Where the crafty villain roams ;
That detectives are but mortal
  Was not meant for Sherlock Holmes.

Lives of pirate kings remind us
  Honesty's a dreadful bore ;
Therefore let the future find us
  Revelling in seas of gore.

Of the hero's latest caper,
  And the lovely heroine's fate,
I must—until next week's paper—
  Learn to keep serene and wait.

BROWNING, who was fond of elliptical anecdotes :—

Days ago—I think some ten 'tis—Eh ! what,
  think it's longer :
Scusaterni—*Das ist unrecht*—phew, that " preparation " !
Well, *verb sap sat:* In the future make the
  trousers stronger
(Thanks—*des bonbons*—*confettura*—now for the
  narration) :—

Theory: solving Euclid Riders;
Practice: drawing wasps and spiders
(Bob, I think, was feeding silkworms),
Ancient Whackem comes up gently,
I—on drawing fixed intently—
Looked up; saw him — cane descends — squirms!!!
And then... you know... pish! Howl? Why should I?
Well—*Adieu*—*Buon giorno*—Good-bye!

KEATS, who received a hamper, celebrates the event in a sonnet :—

The hamper's gone, and all its sweets are gone,
Sweet apples, jam, and toothsome gingerbread;
Soft jennetings—so plentiful this morn
To nourish boyish frames have quickly sped.
Jack's pearly teeth caressed my dark rich cake
—With plump, embedded currants—made at home,
Then drank my ginger-beer of best home make,
A bubbling font of aromatic foam.
Now all have vanished at approach of eve,
And the tired palate sated craves for rest;

Nor for another hamper shall I grieve,
While friends and foes assist with so much zest.
Let slumbrous-lidded sleep descend once more,
And curtain off my comrade's tiresome snore.

HOOD, who was a Cricket enthusiast :—

    Good Mr. Scorer, tell me pray,
        The reason for my luck,
    I'm sure 'tis very foul to-day,
        That I have made a " duck."

    The boy whose bowling made me quail,
        He did a wicket deed ;
    Since he deprived me of the bail
        Of which I stood in need.

    For " driving " I'd a subtle plan,
        But walking came too soon ;
    I never was a ladies' man,
        And yet they say I " spoon."

    One run I got, and that a bye ;
        I felt extremely sold ;
    While never very brave, yet I
        Soon—much too soon—get bowled.

Though otherwise intensely frank,
  My bowling's underhand ;
As Captain I should be a crank,
  Though as a "boss" I'm grand.

Although of poor athletic fame,
  Yet cricket gives me fun ;
For, oh! it is a splendid game
  On which to vilely pun !

REFLECTIONS OF A POETASTER.

(After Calverley.)

SOME love to tune the poet's golden lyre,
  To gaily warble or to sadly chant;
And I to shine as melodist aspire,
                    But can't.

'Tis often said that inspiration comes
When it is least expected—at chance times;
I sit for hours gnawing at my thumbs,
                    For Rhymes.

O for a ready Muse! a facile pen!
Will thought and metre wed? I fear they won't.
Some eyes in a "fine phrenzy" roll; but then,
                    Mine don't.

I wrote—that is, the lamp of verse I lit,
Called the book "Gleanings"; bade the scoffer
    laugh;
The scoffer *did* and rudely spoke of it
                    As chaff.

I penned my preface to the "cultured" mind,
Said I eschewed "mere fame" ('twas scarcely
    true);
Alas! my "gentle readers"—though refined—
                    Were few.

No "long-felt want" my poems could supply,
Though type and binding both were of the best,
It never sold. Yet it was published "By
                    Request."

'Twas by request of fairest Amabel,
She thought the poems "sweet," their meaning
    "deep";
Was it their depth when over them she fell
                    Asleep?

The surest way to glory, you'll allow,
Is to create a cult, to found a "school,"
They'll call me genius then who deem me now
                    A fool.

Till then I cherish up this thought sublime,
Though not much comfort—yet it is a crumb;
With the stage villain I predict, " A time
　　　　　　　Will come! "

UNWIN BROTHERS, THE GRESHAM PRESS, CHILWORTH AND LONDON.

NOVELS PUBLISHED BY A. D. INNES & COMPANY BEDFORD ST. MDCCCXCV.

NOVELS AND FICTION PUBLISHED BY A. D. INNES & CO.

NEW ONE-VOLUME NOVELS.

THREE NEW NOVELS OF ADVENTURE.

By FRANK BARRETT, Author of "The Admirable Lady Biddy Fane."

A Set of Rogues: Namely, Christopher Sutton, John Dawson, the Señor don Sanchez del Castillo de Castelaña, and Moll Dawson. Their Wicked Conspiracy, and a True Account of their Travels and Adventures.

With Illustrations by S. COWELL. Crown 8vo, buckram, 6s.

By JAMES CHALMERS.

The Renegade.

Being a Novel dealing chiefly with the Career of the American Captain Paul Jones.

With Illustrations by JOHN WILLIAMSON. Crown 8vo, buckram, 6s.

By J. C. SNAITH.

Mistress Dorothy Marvin.

A Tale of the Seventeenth Century. Being Excerpta from the Memoirs of Sir Edward Armstrong, Baronet, of Copeland Hall, in the County of Somerset.

With Illustrations by S. COWELL. Crown 8vo, buckram, 6s.

By ARTHUR RICKETT.

Lost Chords. Being Some Emotions without Morals.

Crown 8vo, cloth, 2s. 6d. net.

New Novels—*continued.*

By LESLIE KEITH, Author of "The Chilcotes," "Lisbeth," etc.
For Love of Prue.
Crown 8vo, cloth, 6s.

By the late Mrs. J. K. SPENDER, Author of "Thirteen Doctors," etc.
The Wooing of Doris.
Crown 8vo, cloth, 6s.

NEW AND CHEAPER EDITIONS OF POPULAR NOVELS.

By ANTHONY HOPE.
Half a Hero.
New and cheaper edition, crown 8vo, cloth, 3s. 6d.

"The fashion through which he presents his people and his ideas is exceedingly bright and vivacious, marked with that peculiar ease and adequacy of expression which he and one or two more of our modern novelists have made their own."—*Athenæum.*

"An atmosphere where energetic vitality seems indigenous, and all conversations bristle with enough humour, epigrammatic point, and caustic but good-natured satire, to make dullness impossible."—*Spectator.*

"The plot is far less artificial than is usual in political novels: the dialogue is unaffected, crisp, and witty; the actors are skilfully individualized."—*Times.*

By FRANKFORT MOORE.
Two in the Bush and Others Elsewhere.
Crown 8vo, cloth, 3s. 6d.

"All the six stories are fresh and bright, and display the writer's undoubted versatility."—*Vanity Fair.*

"Contains one very remarkable story, and is good throughout."—*The World.*

"Carry the reader on from page to page until criticism is forgotten in enjoyment."—*Daily Graphic.*

"For raciness and strong masculine humour Mr. Moore has written nothing better."—*Birmingham Gazette.*

By RICHARD PRYCE.
Winifred Mount.
Crown 8vo, cloth, 6s.

"The merit and charm do not depend upon plot or incident, but upon the author's appreciation of character. Truth to life is recognized in all the well-painted miniatures that fill his pages."—*Spectator.*

"A very entertaining and well-written novel of society. The likeness of the plot, and the daintiness with which the life and character are filled in, make the interest lively and effervescent."—*Birmingham Post.*

By DOROTHEA GERARD.
Lot 13.
Crown 8vo, cloth, 6s.

"Delightfully fresh and original in plot, character, and incident, and it has the charm that Miss Gerard's work never lacks of an atmosphere of imagination and poetry."—*Guardian.*

"Will help to sustain the reputation of Miss Gerard."—*Speaker.*

"Altogether a more than usually well managed novel."—*Literary World.*

RECENT SIX SHILLING NOVELS.

By Stanley Weyman.

My Lady Rotha.

A Romance of the Thirty Years' War. With 8 Illustrations by John Williamson. Crown 8vo, buckram, 6s.

"No one who begins will lay it down before the end, it is so extremely well carried on from adventure to adventure."—*Saturday Review.*

"A novel which everybody must read and enjoy as such books are meant to be read and enjoyed."—*Speaker.*

"Holds the reader's interest captive from beginning to end."—*Manchester Guardian.*

"Exhibits in high degree and ample abundance the qualities which have so certainly and so fast brought Mr. Weyman to the front; the excellence of the narrative style, the skill with which the historical element is introduced, the adequacy for romantic purposes of the character drawing, and above all the quick invention in incident and situation."—*St. James's Gazette.*

"As good as, if not better than, any of his previous books. Scene after scene rises before us all vivid, all excellent, but so much better when fitted into the whole than extracted that we shall leave readers to find them for themselves."—*Guardian.*

"A capital story, full of stir and movement, with vivid description and happy characterization."—*Spectator.*

By the late Mrs. J. K. Spender.

Thirteen Doctors.

Crown 8vo, cloth, 6s.

"Mrs. Spender's stories will be read by many who will find them highly exciting."—*Realm.*

"Anybody desiring a companionable volume for a railway journey is likely to find his requirements met by 'Thirteen Doctors.'"—*Spectator.*

"Cannot but be welcomed."—*Daily Telegraph.*

"For variety and freshness of subject, perfect polish, and naturalness of style, the stories are unique."—*Sheffield Telegraph.*

"A collection of capital stories which in spite of the title are by no means of the stock medical sensational kind."—*Glasgow Herald.*

"A book that we can heartily recommend to our readers as having between its covers something more than the mere excited interest usually connected with the modern short story."—*Liverpool Mercury.*

By Dorothea Gerard.

Lot 13.

Crown 8vo, cloth, 6s.

"A bright, buoyant, bustling story, with plenty of local colour derived from the scenery and the society, black and white, of a West Indian plantation."—*Times.*

Recent 6s. Novels—*continued*.

By RICHARD PRYCE.

The Burden of a Woman.

Crown 8vo, cloth, price 6s.

"This is a very finished and admirable piece of work. Every character is drawn and every incident presented with exceeding great care, but there are no obtrusive signs of painstaking. Mr. Richard Pryce already holds a high place among novelists. 'The Burden of a Woman' will give him a higher position still."—*Daily Chronicle.*

"Mr. Richard Pryce has worked a fresh vein of realistic romance, and has done so with eminent success. The story which the author has here presented so artistically is both a powerful and a beautiful one told with mingled strength and delicacy, enriched with admirable character-drawing, and marked by real distinction of tone and style. Mr. Pryce has conferred a benefit upon novel readers by the production of so noble and interesting a book as 'The Burden of a Woman.'"—*Speaker.*

"Mr. Richard Pryce's latest book is also, we think, his best."—*Daily News.*

"The reputation of Mr. Richard Pryce will be strengthened and broadened by his latest novel. We fully expect 'The Burden of a Woman' to survive as one of the best novels of the year."—*Birmingham Post.*

"This novel is good to read. . . . Mr. Pryce, we fancy, has done nothing better than 'The Burden of a Woman.'"—*Birmingham Gazette.*

"By dint of work of exceptional merit Mr. Richard Pryce has attained a very distinct position as a novelist. His last novel, 'The Burden of a Woman,' is his best. . . . There is something greater than mere talent. Mr. Pryce has set himself a difficult precedent."—*Star.*

By the same Author.

Winifred Mount.

Crown 8vo, cloth, 6s. *New Edition.*

By DEAS CROMARTY, Author of "A High Little World," etc.

Under God's Sky.

Crown 8vo, cloth, 6s.

"A very powerful and fascinating dramatic tale. . . . Always strong and intense. The plot . . . is intensely interesting."—*Scotsman.*

"We always welcome Deas Cromarty's books; they are unlike those of any other writer and better than those of very many contemporary novelists."—*Daily Chronicle.*

"It is a long time since we have read a book which affords greater pleasure than the one now under notice. . . . An exceedingly clever piece of work."—*The Manchester Courier.*

"Is undoubtedly a novel with a backbone, and will repay those who take the trouble to study it as carefully as it is written."—*St. James's Gazette.*

"In the best sense one of the most successful stories which have appeared this season; it gives such evidence of power that we shall look with peculiar interest for further work by the same writer."—*Observer.*

By CAROLINE C. HOLROYD.

Seething Days.

A Romance of Tudor Times. With 8 Illustrations by JOHN WILLIAMSON. Crown 8vo, cloth, 6s.

"For a picture of the age the book is admirable, and we congratulate the author upon her facility in catching its tone and manners."—*Pall Mall Gazette.*

"A very cleverly written romance of the sixteenth century. A book that should be very popular."—*The Lady.*

"A very interesting and admirable piece of historical fiction."—*Morning Leader.*

POPULAR NOVELS.

Crown 8vo, uniform scarlet cloth, 3s. 6d. *each Volume.*

By ANTHONY HOPE, Author of "The Prisoner of Zenda."
Half a Hero.
Crown 8vo, cloth, 3s. 6d. *New Edition.*

"The book is delightful to read, and an excellent piece of work."—*Standard.*

Mr. Witt's Widow.
Crown 8vo, cloth, 3s. 6d.

"A brilliant little tale. . . . Exhibits unborrowed ingenuity, plausibility, and fertility in surprises."—*Times.*

"Excellent fooling. From first to last the story is keenly and quietly amusing."—*Scotsman.*

By C. R. COLERIDGE.
Amethyst.
The Story of a Beauty. Crown 8vo, cloth, 3s. 6d.

"Extremely amusing, interesting, and brightly written."—*Guardian.*

"Clever in its analysis, pleasant in its diction, and artistic in its presentment of certain aspects of fashionable humanity."—*National Observer.*

"We do not think that we have seen any work by this author stronger or more interesting."—*Speaker.*

By F. FRANKFORT MOORE.
Two in the Bush and Others Elsewhere.
Crown 8vo, cloth, 3s. 6d. *New Edition.*

"Carry the reader on from page to page till criticism is forgotten in enjoyment."—*Daily Graphic.*

By "NUMQUAM."
A Son of the Forge.
By ROBERT BLATCHFORD. New and Cheaper Edition. Crown 8vo, cloth, 3s. 6d.

"Nor Tolstoi nor Zola have written anything more vividly descriptive of the horror of war than the powerful realism of life in the trenches before Sebastopol, which will for ever render famous Mr. Robert Blatchford's story."—*Sheffield Telegraph.*

"If not a genuine bit of autobiography, it has all the realism and verisimilitude of one. The plain truth of it, and the unaffected force and sincerity of its unadorned style and phraseology, are merits of no mean order."—*Scotsman.*

"A rattling good story. It is well and powerfully told, with an occasional flash of humour in situation and dialogue, and possesses a strong readable interest which inclines one to read straight on, having once commenced, until the book is finished."—*Literary World.*

"Not for many a day have we read descriptions so terse and yet so true. The story itself is simple, but decidedly fresh and novel and human."—*Bradford Observer.*

POPULAR 3s. 6d. NOVELS.

By E. GERARD, Joint-Author of "Reata."

The Voice of a Flower.

Crown 8vo, cloth, 3s. 6d.

"A novel of which one can speak justly only in superlatives. It is as perfect in its beauty as the carnation about which we read so much in the story."—*Liverpool Mercury.*

"A fantastic but graceful romance. The mystic, legendary story of the Ronsecco carnation is skilfully wrought into the plot."—*Speaker.*

"This romantic story, well and cleverly told, is singularly unlike the run of modern fiction."—*Manchester Courier.*

"Recounted with infinite pathos, grace of style, and delicacy of feeling."—*Daily Telegraph.*

"A charming story."—*Academy.*

By a New Author.

6,000 Tons of Gold.

A Romance of Hard Cash. Crown 8vo, cloth, 3s. 6d.

"The extremely clever author has worked out the disabilities of a billionaire even more artistically ... has beaten Godwin out of the field with the skill with which he has devised his plot."—*Spectator.*

"The idea is ingenious and the development no less so."—*Morning Post.*

"Presents a deeply interesting study as well as an exciting story."—*Glasgow Herald.*

By ROMA WHITE.

Punchinello's Romance.

Crown 8vo, cloth, 3s. 6d.

"We give Roma White the warmest of welcomes into the world of fiction. . . . Admirably and irresistibly comic, without anything in the nature of force or even of apparent exaggeration, ready at the least moment to run into equally true pathos."—*Graphic.*

"A charming little story. There are readers who like to be made to laugh and readers who like to be made to cry, and this book is calculated to meet both."—*Black and White.*

By FERGUS MACKENZIE.

The Humours of Glenbruar.

New Edition. Crown 8vo, cloth, price 3s. 6d.

"He has the same command over the springs of laughter and tears that Barrie and Crockett and Ian Maclaren have, and this work, which in its origin owes nothing to either, is fit in quality to rank with any of those noble names."—*Morning Leader.*

"Mr. Mackenzie must have gone directly to the hearts and homes of the Angus folk to be able to interpret so truthfully and touchingly their cares and sorrows as well as their humours."—*Scotsman.*

By JOHN CUNNINGHAM.

Broomieburn: Border Sketches.

Crown 8vo, buckram, gilt top, 3s. 6d.

"Will prove delightful reading."—*Morning Post.*

"One of the least pretentious, but at the same time most quietly effective, books dealing with Scotch life of yesterday that have recently appeared."—*Spectator.*

"Contains old traits and memories that are worthy preserving; they have been gathered by a hand that has been guided by an observant eye and a sympathetic mind."—*Scotsman.*

www.ingramcontent.com/pod-product-compliance
Lightning Source LLC
Chambersburg PA
CBHW031401160426
43196CB00007B/845